My Book by Me

DISCARD

Written and Illustrated
by Dana Meachen Rau

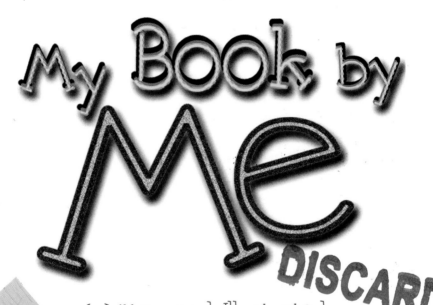

Children's Press ®
A Division of Grolier Publishing
New York • London • Hong Kong • Sydney
Danbury, Connecticut

For Mom and Dad, who always urged me to be creative
and didn't mind when I drew on the walls of the garage.
–D. M. R.

Reading Consultants
Linda Cornwell
Coordinator of School Quality and Professional Improvement
(Indiana State Teachers Association)

Katharine A. Kane
Education Consultant
(Retired, San Diego County Office of Education and San Diego State University)

Visit Children's Press® on the Internet at:
http://publishing.grolier.com

Library of Congress Cataloging-in-Publication Data
Rau, Dana Meachen.
     My book by me / written and illustrated by Dana Meachen Rau.
          p. cm. — (Rookie reader)
     Summary: A child describes the pleasures and freedom of writing one's
own book and then reading it as well.
     ISBN 0-516-22032-2 (lib. bdg.)   0-516-27082-6 (pbk.)
     [1. Authorship—Fiction. 2. Books and reading—Fiction.] I. Title. II. Series.
PZ7+
[E]—dc21   99-057167

GROLIER
PUBLISHING

I'm making my own book.
It's by me!

3

My book can have big words

dinosaur

or little words.

cat

I can write in

BLUE

or

Red

or

Yellow

or

GREEN.

I can be anything in my book—
silly,

quiet,

scared,

brave.

I can be a bug,
a bear,
or just a kid.

I can wear anything in my book—
a firefighter hat,

clown shoes,

or red suspenders,
a purple bow tie,
and polka-dot socks!

17

I can go anywhere in my book—

inside,

outside,

to the zoo,

or on a picnic.

I can fill my book
with everything,

or nothing at all.

I like to read
my book by me.

My friends like to read

my book by me, too!

Word List (63 words)

a	clown	like	scared
all	everything	little	shoes
and	fill	making	silly
anything	firefighter	me	socks
anywhere	friends	my	suspenders
at	go	nothing	the
be	green	on	tie
bear	hat	or	to
big	have	outside	too
blue	I	own	wear
book	I'm	picnic	with
bow	in	polka-dot	words
brave	inside	purple	write
bug	it's	quiet	yellow
by	just	read	zoo
can	kid	red	

About the Author

Dana Meachen Rau is the author of many books for children, including *A Box Can Be Many Things*, *Hands*, *Feet*, and *Bob's Vacation* (which she also illustrated) in the Rookie Reader series. Dana also works as a children's book editor and lives with her husband, Chris, and son, Charlie, in Farmington, Connecticut.

While making this book, Dana used lots of different items from around her house—paper, foam, fabric, magazines, yarn, felt, paint chips, crayons, markers, and cardboard. Try to make your own book by you. It's fun (and sometimes messy) and makes a perfect item for show-and-tell.